Ele
Nickel Silver,
Old Sheffield Plate
and Close Plate
Makers' Marks
from 1784

EPNS
Electroplated Nickel Silver, Old Sheffield Plate and Close Plate Makers' Marks
from 1784

George Mappin

foulsham
LONDON • NEW YORK • TORONTO • SYDNEY

foulsham

The Publishing House, Bennetts Close,
Cippenham, Berkshire, SL1 5AP, England

ISBN-13: 978-0-572-03190-9
ISBN-10: 0-572-03190-4

Printed by St Edmundsbury Press Ltd,
Bury St Edmunds, Suffolk

CONTENTS

OLD SHEFFIELD PLATE AND ELECTROPLATE

One of the problems with identifying plated items is that there is no single source of information on the makers' marks. Add to this the fact that some marks are not registered at all and checking every mark becomes impossible. Therefore, while every effort has been made to ensure accuracy, it is not possible to go back to source to verify every mark.

Old Sheffield Plate

Old Sheffield Plate was made by a different process from electroplate and the marks referring to Old Sheffield Plate are indicated in the book by (OSP).

Old Sheffield Plate was invented in the middle of the eighteenth century and its manufacture continued until about the 1860s, by which time electroplating was well established. It was made by fusing a layer of silver on to copper. The designs used by the manufacturers were copied from popular silverware and much Old Sheffield Plate was made by silversmiths. The plate has a faint glow with a blueish tinge and is less dull than electroplated silver.

The words 'Best Sheffield Heavy Plating' were only used after 1820. Between 1773 and 1784 Old Sheffield plate has no marks as manufacturers were forbidden to mark their goods to prevent them from passing them off as silver. Later items, however, may also not carry a mark.

'Sheffield Plated' is only used on electroplated items.

Close Plate

Close plating was the only way of silver plating steel. Electroplating steel was not successful because the adverse reaction of the electrolyte on the base metal made it rust.

The article was made in steel and completely finished. It was then dipped in sal ammoniac, which acted as a flux, and then into molten tin, so that it was completely covered.

Silver foil was cut into the shape of the article and put into position. A heated soldering iron was then rubbed over its surface, causing the underlying tin to melt and unite the silver and steel.

Close plating was a Sheffield and Birmingham trade. Samuel Roberts, a Sheffield manufacturer, took out a patent for the manufacture of Close Plate spoons and forks in 1789, but most of the items found now date from the nineteenth century or the period up to 1914. The main items made in Close Plate were those which required more strength than would be found in Old Sheffield Plate. They include spurs, buckles, candlesnuffers, nutcrackers, skewers, marrow scoops, fish slices and, of course, dessert knife blades, ladles, spoons and scissors.

Most Close Plate items are marked. An Act of Parliament of 1784 laid down that Old Sheffield Platers and Close Platers working in Sheffield and an area of 100 miles radius around it (which included Birmingham) had to register their marks at the Sheffield Assay Office.

Records are complete until the mid 1830s when this Act became a dead letter. Close Platers' marks usually consist of a number of different shields containing the maker's initials and registered device, sometimes struck twice, and the letters PS for plated steel.

Electroplate

Electroplating or silver plating was perfected in 1842 by Elkington & Co. of Birmingham. Articles made of copper, Britannia metal, nickel silver, nickel, brass or British plate were used as the base and coated with a layer of pure silver. The item to be plated was attached to a negative pole and submerged in a solution of potassium cyanide. The positive pole was attached to a 100 per cent pure silver sheet. A low-voltage current was then passed through the solution. The silver sheets acted as a cathode producing silver ions which passed into the solution. These were drawn to the article, acting as an anode, adhering to its surface. A thicker layer was produced the longer the article was immersed in the charged solution. The quality of the product is partly dependent on how clean the Portland cement-lined vat containing the solution was kept, as foreign bodies in the solution caused imperfections in the plating. Once removed from the solution, the article was hammered over its surface to ensure that the silver coating had adhered properly, then burnished.

Many manufactuers of Old Sheffield Plate moved over to the new process and marked their wares with their stamp. In general, marked English EPNS is from Sheffield, while unmarked English EPNS is from Birmingham. However, usually only the teapot in a teaset was marked so do not be misled by unmarked cups, etc.

Base Metals

Nickel Silver
An alloy of copper, zinc and nickel, nickel silver was discovered to be the best base for electroplating and is still used today. Worn areas show the base metal as silvery-grey. Items often have EPNS or EPGS (electroplated German silver, named as nickel was first mined in Saxony) stamped on the base; or they may display EP, NS or GS.

British Plate is a form of nickel silver and BP is usually marked on the base of goods made of British Plate.

Copper
A popular base metal at the beginning of electroplating, copper became less popular as it was softer than nickel silver and because when the silver coating began to wear away, the base metal showed through as an unsightly orangey-red.. Silver-plated copper wares are usually from the early to mid Victorian period and often have EP stamped on the base.

Britannia Metal
Britannia metal is a form of hard pewter developed about 1770 as a cheap alternative to Old Sheffield Plate. It was then found that it made a good base for electroplating and plating on Britannia metal started in 1845. By 1870, however, the increasing burden of labour costs led to the production of poor quality wares made of thin gauge metal

with only a light coating of silver. After 1855, EPBM is often stamped on the base of Britannia metal items. Pewter goods are collectible in their own right.

Design Registration Marks

Some metal wares may be dated approximately if their design was registered.

Diamond Registration Marks

A diamond-shaped impressed registration mark dates the article as 1843-83 or an impressed registration number from 1884.

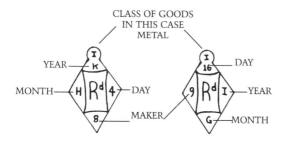

Year Letter Codes 1842-67

A	1845	J	1854	S	1849
B	1858	K	1857	T	1867
C	1844	L	1856	U	1848
D	1852	M	1859	V	1850
E	1855	N	1864	W	1865
F	1847	O	1862	X	1842
G	1863	P	1851	Y	1853
H	1843	Q	1866	Z	1860
I	1846	R	1861		

Year Letter Codes for 1868-83

A	1871	I	1872	U	1874
C	1870	J	1880	V	1876
D	1878	K	1883	W	1878
E	1881	L	1882	X	1868
F	1873	P	1877	Z	1879
H	1869	S	1875		

Months

The months were the same for both series.

A	December (except 1860)
B	October
C	January
D	September
E	May
G	February
H	April
I	July
K	November and December 1860
M	June
O	January
R	August and 1–19 September 1957
W	March

Date

The date of the month was marked simply as the number.

Registration Numbers

From 1884, registration numbers took over from the diamond registration mark.

1884	1–19753	1895	246975–268391
1885	19754–40479	1896	268392–291240
1886	40480–64519	1897	291241–311657
1887	64520–90482	1898	311658–331706
1888	90483–116647	1899	331707–351201
1889	116648–141272	1900–09	35120–550999
1890	141273–163766	1910–19	552000–673749
1891	163767–185712	1920–29	673750–751159
1892	185713–205239	1930–39	751160–837519
1893	205240–224719	1940–49	837520–860853
1894	224720–246974		

Makers' and Other Marks

Knowing the maker can help to establish the date of an article as you can ascertain when that company was producing goods.

Most Sheffield platers stamped their initials on to their wares, but some used their surname or full name. In order to mimic sterling silver, makers often punched their initials in a sequence of four punches, and marks were usually in intaglio, that is punched with the letters in relief. If they did not have the required number of initials, they would commonly add a fourth, often 'S', at the end.

Some marks use an 'I' instead of a 'J' in the company initials.

Trade Marks
Trade marks could be registered from about 1878.

A1
This is stamped on some wares to indicate the best quality but has no real significance.

Electroplated
Sometimes stamped on electroplated wares.

England or Made in England
'England' is commonly found on goods between 1890 and 1920 but never before that time.

'Made in England' is sometimes found on goods made after about 1920.

Crown inside a Shield
This denotes that a product was made before 1897. It was designed to mimic the Sheffield silver crown but its use was banned in about 1897.

Numbers or Letters

A single number may denote the capacity in half pints, although it can also denote a variation in size or a particular style or even the workman's number. A single or pair of letters are frequently the workman's initials.

HOW TO USE THIS BOOK

This book is designed to help you identify marks found on EPNS and Old Sheffield Plate. The organisation of the information is based on the fact that the mark itself is your starting point.

The marks are not necessarily shown to scale. In some cases, detail has been lost due to wear and tear. Different companies with the same surname may or may not be related.

Old Sheffield Plate is marked (OSP).

Close Plate is marked (CP).

The marks have been organised in two sections.

The first section includes all those marks which contain initials, names or words.

- The marks under each letter are listed with the initials first, in alphabetical order where relevant, followed by the names and words in alphabetical order.
- Where the mark contains initials and one of those initials is clearly dominant, the mark has been listed under the dominant letter.
- Where the mark contains initials and none is dominant, the mark has been listed under the first initial letter, reading from left to right. This is because the initials do not always relate readily to the maker's actual name.
- Where a full name is provided in the mark, it has been listed under the initial letter of the surname.

The second section contains marks which are purely pictorial and contain neither initials nor names. They are grouped into images with a similar theme, then into alphabetical order by the name of that general type of image, such as 'bell' or 'hand'.

Charles James Allen &
Sidney Darwin
Sheffield
1893 ...

Charles James Allen &
Sidney Darwin
Sheffield
1879 c. ...

Charles James Allen &
Sidney Darwin
Sheffield
1893 ...

Armstrong & Scott
Birmingham
1894 ...

T. Aston & Son
Birmingham
1893 ...

A.J. Beardshaw & Co.
Sheffield
1893 ...

A. Beardshaw & Co.
Sheffield
1869 ...

Alfred Browett
Birmingham
1855 c. – 1896

Browett, Ashberry &
Co.
Birmingham
1897 ...

A.J. Beardshaw & Co.
Sheffield
1893 ...

A. Beardshaw & Co.
Sheffield
1879 c. ...

Briddon Brothers
*Victoria Plate Works,
Sheffield*

Atkin Brothers
Sheffield
1853 ...

Ashforth Ellis & Co.
Sheffield
1770   (OSP)

Arthur E. Furniss
Sheffield
1870 c. ...

George Bowen & Sons
Birmingham
1890 c. ...

Francis Higgins Jr;
Portland Co. Ltd
London & Clapton Mills
1859–1867

Martin Brothers & Co.
Sheffield

 A. Hatfield
Sheffield
1808 (CP)

 Thomas H. Daniel &
Thomas R. Arter
Birmingham
1882 c.–1896

 Jehoiada Alsop Rhodes
Sheffield
1872 c.–1888 c.

 Silber & Fleming
London
1884–1898

   Silber & Fleming
London
1884–1898

 Arthur Willis
Sheffield
1897 …

 Henry Williamson
London

 H. Schurhoff & Co.
Birmingham

 Hills, Menke & Co.
Birmingham

Lee & Wigfull
John Street Works,
Sheffield

ALBION SILVER

Thomas Aldridge
London
1865 c. ...

**THOMAS ALDRIDGE
57 BROMPTON ROAD
LONDON**

Societe Anonyme des
Converts Alfenide
Paris

John Round & Sons Ltd
Sheffield
1880 c ...

James Allan & Co.
Sheffield
1849–1855

James Allan
Sheffield
1855–1872

**JAMES ALLAN
SHEFFIELD**

J. Allgood
Sheffield
1812   (CP)

E. Allport
Sheffield
1812   (CP)

Joseph Gilbert
Sun Works,
Birmingham

	Harrison Brothers & Howson *Sheffield* 1898 c ...
	Viners *Sheffield* 1925–1974
	Daniel & Arter *Globe Nevada Silver Works, Birmingham*
	Rosing Brothers & Co. *London*
	Perry & Company Ltd *Birmingham*
ANGLE 25 PLATE	William Hutton & Sons *Sheffield* 1886 c.–1893
ARCAS	Cowper-Coles, Cowper Bickerton *London*
	Daniel & Arter *Globe Nevada Silver Works, Birmingham*
ARGENTINA SILVER *Joseph Gilbert*	Joseph Gilbert *Sun Works, Birmingham*

Gilding & Silvering Co.
Middlesex

ARGOSY SILVER

Solomon Lewis Gorer
Middlesex

ARGOSY SILVER

Arnold & Lewis
Manchester
1875 c. ...

ARNOLD&LEWIS MANCHESTER

Philip Ashberry
Sheffield
1845 c.–1855

PHILIP ASHBERRY SHEFFIELD

Philip Ashberry & Sons
Sheffield
1856–1860 c.

PHILIP ASHBERRY&SONS BEST ELECTRO PLATE SHEFFIELD

Philip Ashberry & Sons
Sheffield
1861 ...

PHILIP ASHBERRY&SONS SHEFFIELD

Philip Ashberry & Sons
Sheffield

Philip Ashberry & Sons
Sheffield
1861–1915

G. Ashforth & Co.
Sheffield
1784   (OSP)

	Ashley *Sheffield* 1816	
	Askew *Nottingham* 1828	
	Atkin Brothers *Sheffield* 20th Century	
	Perry & Co. Ltd *Birmingham*	

Broadhead & Atkin
Sheffield
1846–1853

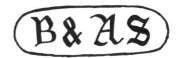

Biddle & Collingwood
Birmingham
1875 ...

Brookes & Crookes
Atlantic Works
Sheffield (cutlery only)

Brown & Clark
Birmingham

Benetfink & Co.
London
1895 c...

Boulton & Fothergill
Birmingham
1764

Boardman, Glossop & Co.
Sheffield
1847–1894

Boardman, Glossop & Co.
Sheffield & London
1895 ...

Boardman, Glossop & Co.
Clarence Works
Sheffield

Henry Bourne &
Daniel J. O'Neill
Birmingham
1881–1886

Henry Arthur Goodall
London

Barker Brothers
Birmingham
1886–1896

Briddon Brothers
Victoria Plate Works
Sheffield

Briddon Brothers
Sheffield
1863–1910

Chantrill & Co.
Birmingham

The Birmingham Guild
of Handicrafts Ltd
Birmingham
1897 ...

Barnett Henry
Abrahams
London
1890 ...

B.J. Round & Sons
Birmingham
1900 ...

James Pinder & Co.
Sheffield
1877–1894

Badger, Worrall &
Armitage
Sheffield

Bingley, George Bower
Sheffield

Ihlee & Horne
London

W. Banister
Birmingham
1808

Silverston, Isaac & Co.
Birmingham

Henry Barnascone
Sheffield
1868 c.–1883 c.

Henry Barnascone & Son
Sheffield
1884 ...

Barnet

Z.BARRACLOUGH&SONS LEEDS	Z. Barraclough & Sons *Leeds* 1887 ...
	H. Samuel & Sons *Manchester*
	Beach & Minte *Birmingham*
	G. Beldon *Sheffield* 1809
	Beldon, Hoyland & Co. *Sheffield* 1785
BENETFINK&CO CHEAPSIDE	Benetfink & Co. *London* 1880 c ...
	J.W. Benson *London*
	Daniel & Arter *Globe Nevada Silver Works, Birmingham*
	H. Best *Sheffield* 1814

Best & Wastidge
Sheffield
1816

Henry Biggin & Co.
Sheffield
1880–1884

W. Bingley
Sheffield
1787

Birts & Son
Woolwich

Thomas Bishop
Sheffield
1830

Arthur Culf
Sheffield

William Page & Co.
Birmingham

Slack & Grinold
Bath Works, Sheffield

M. Boulton & Co.
Birmingham
1784

BOVAL

James Woolley, Sons & Co.
Manchester

Joseph Bradshaw
Birmingham
1822 c.

J. Bradshaw
Birmingham
1822

Daniel & Arter
*Globe Nevada Silver
Works, Birmingham*

**BRENADA SILVER
J. R. McC.**

James Robert
McClelland
Sheffield

**WM BRIGGS&Co
SHEFFIELD**

William Briggs & Co.
Sheffield
1876–1900

Atkinson Brothers
Mill Works, Sheffield

Philip Ashberry &
Sons
Sheffield
1861 ...

Browett, Ashberry &
Co.
Birmingham

Browett, Ashberry & Co.
Birmingham
1897 ...

Benjamin Grayson &
Son
Sheffield
1871 ...

Brittain, Wilkinson &
Brownhill
Sheffield
1785   (OSP)

Broadhead & Atkin
Sheffield
1843–1853

Rogers Broadhead & Co.
Sheffield
1853–1900

Cooper Brothers &
Sons Ltd
Sheffield
1867–1964

Joseph Brown
Sheffield
1849–1867

Brumby & Middleton
Sheffield
1889–1897

Daniel & Arter
*Globe Nevada Silver
Works, Birmingham*

John Moreton & Co.
Wolverhampton,
Sheffield & London

T. Butts
Birmingham
1807 c.

BUXTON &
RUSSELL

Edwin James Buxton
& Samuel Russell
Sheffield
1852–1860

Joseph Elliot & Sons
Sheffield
1890 c ...

Creswick & Company
Sheffield

Carnelly & Co.
Birmingham
1867–1885 c.

Creswick & Co.
Sheffield
1855 c.–1887

Creswick & Co.
Sheffield
1863–1887

Culf & Kay
Sheffield
... 1896

C. Boardman
Sheffield

Roberts
Sheffield
1879–1892

Cooper Brothers &
Sons Ltd
Sheffield
1895 c. ...

George Edwards
Glasgow

Charles Ellis & Co.
Sheffield

Muirhead & Arthur
Glasgow
1883 c. ...

Charles Howard
Collins
Birmingham
1889 ...

Hawksworth, Eyre &
Co.
Sheffield
1850 c. ...

Cartwright, Hirons &
Woodward
Birmingham
1853–1859

Christopher Johnson
& Co.
Sheffield
1896 ...

Levesley Brothers
*Central Works,
Sheffield*

Sissons
Sheffield
1855–1891

Lockwood Brothers Ltd.
Sheffield
1898 c. ...

Levetus Brothers
Birmingham

Hawksworth, Eyre &
Co. Ltd
Sheffield
1900 c. ...

J. F. Causer
Sheffield
1824

(OSP)

Thomas S. Richards & Co.
Birmingham

T. Cheston
Sheffield
1809

(OSP)

T. Child
Sheffield
1812

(OSP)

Christofle & Company
Paris

Land
Sheffield
1920–1944

TRADE CIVIC MARK
E. P. B. M.

	Land *Sheffield* 1945–1977
CLARKE'S PATENT	John Clarke & Sons *Sheffield* 1895 ...
CLARKS **JUBILEE GOLD**	John Clark *Birmingham*
	W. Coldwell *Sheffield* 1806
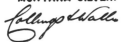 	Collings & Wallace *Birmingham*
	George Richmond Collis & Co. *Birmingham & London* 1873–1893
	John Shaw & Sons, Ltd. *Wolverton*
COPE	C. G. Cope *Sheffield* 1817
	J. Corn & J. Sheppard *Birmingham* 1819

33

Joseph Deakin & Sons
Sheffield
1856–1864

J. Cracknall
Sheffield
1814

Creswick & Co.
Sheffield

CRESWICK & C?

T. & J. Creswick
Sheffield
1811 ...

Judd & Co.
London

THE CYPRUS

 John Gilbert & Co. Ltd
Birmingham & London
1879–1890

 Thomas H. Daniel &
Thomas R. Arter
Birmingham
1897 ...

 Davenport & Bray
Sheffield
1871–1874 c.

 William R. Deykin &
Walter A. Harrison
Birmingham
1895 ...

 Frederick Derry &
Henry Jones
Birmingham
1861–1866

 William R. Deykin &
Sons
Birmingham
1854–1895

 J. Dixon & Sons
Sheffield
1835

 J. Dixon & Sons
Sheffield
1835

 J. Deakin
Sheffield
1855–1891

D. Not attributed 1760 (OSP)	
Dawson & Co. *Birmingham* 1897 …	
Fenton Brothers *Sheffield* 1897–1910 c.	
J. Davis *Sheffield* 1816 (OSP)	
James Deakin & Sons *Sheffield* 1871–1900 c.	JAMES DEAKIN & SONS CUTLERS SHEFFIELD
Joseph Deakin & Sons *Sheffield* 1856–1864	JOSEPH DEAKIN & SONS SHEFFIELD
Joseph Deakin & Sons *Sheffield* 1864–1889	JOSEPH DEAKIN & SONS SPRING STREET WORKS SHEFFIELD
Deakin Smith & Co. *Sheffield* 1785 (OSP)	
Brookes & Cookes *Sheffield*	

T. Dixon & Co.
Sheffield
1784 (OSP)

James Dixon & Sons
Sheffield
1851 ...

James Dixon & Sons
Sheffield
1835 (OSP)

James Dixon & Sons
Sheffield
1879 ...

James Dixon & Sons
Sheffield
1890 c. ...

James Dixon & Sons
Sheffield
1835 c. (OSP)

James Dixon & Sons
Sheffield
1835 (OSP)

James Dixon & Sons
Sheffield
1835 (OSP)

I. Drabble & Co.
Sheffield
1805 (OSP)

G. B. Dunn
Birmingham
1810

Frederick Barnes & Co.
London, Birmingham
& Sheffield

Frederick Barnes & Co.
London, Birmingham
& Sheffield

John James Durrant
London
1874–1897

Elkington & Co.
Birmingham
1840–1897

Elkington & Co.
Birmingham
1898–1899

Elkington & Co.
Birmingham
1900 …

Ellis & Co.
Birmingham
1896 …

Elkington & Co. Ltd
Birmingham

Elkington & Co. Ltd
Birmingham

Elkington & Co. Ltd
Birmingham

Elkington & Co. Ltd
Birmingham
1865 …

E. Bradley
Sheffield

Edwin Blyde & Co.
Sheffield
1872 ...

Arthur E. Furniss
Sheffield
1872 ...

Haseler Brothers
Birmingham
1888 ...

E. J. Makin
Sheffield

Elkington, Mason & Co.
Birmingham

Elkington, Mason & Co.
Birmingham
1842–1864

Mappin Brothers
Queens Works,
Sheffield & London

Mappin Brothers
Queens Works,
Sheffield & London

A. Hodd & Sons
Middlesex

A. Hodd & Sons
Middlesex

 Wilson & Davis
London & Sheffield

 W. R. Humphreys & Co.
Sheffield
1889 c. ...

 Robinson & Company
Sheffield

    Ebenezer Stacey & Sons
Sheffield
1870 c.–1900 c.

 E.S. Wells
Birmingham
1899 ...

T.W. EATON & CO. SHEFFIELD T.W. Eaton & Co.
Sheffield
1899 ...

 EGLENTINE F. Eglington
Staffordshire

Electro-Imperial. F.W. Frederick Whitehouse
Lion Works,
Birmingham

The Potosi Company
Birmingham

Elkington & Co. Ltd
Birmingham
... 1870 c.

Elkington & Co. Ltd
Birmingham

Elkington & Co. Ltd
Birmingham

W. Ellerby
London
1803

Joseph Elliot & Sons
Sheffield
1890 c. ...

Isaac Ellis & Sons
Sheffield

Thomas Turner & Co.
Sheffield
1886 ...

William Hay
Birmingham

 S. Evans
Sheffield
1816

 Evans & Matthews
Birmingham
1890 c. ...

Fenton & Anderton
Sheffield

Fattorini & Sons
*Bradford, Kirkgate
&Westgate*
1895 c. ...

F. Cobb & Co
Sheffield
1905–1911 c.

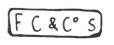

Fenton Brothers Ltd.
Sheffield
1897 ...

Fenton Brothers
Sheffield
1860–1880 c.

Fenton Brothers
Sheffield
1880 c.–1896

Frederick Derry
Birmingham
1867–1891

F.E. Timm & Co.
Sheffield
1877 c. ...

F.E. Timm
Sheffield

Fenton Brothers
Sheffield
1883–1888

 Francis Howard
Sheffield
1890 c. ...

 Howard
Sheffield
1870–1974

 Frederick Wilson &
William Davis
Sheffield
1870–1883

 Farrow & Jackson
London

 Fattorini & Sons
Bradford
1890 c. ...

FOX PROCTOR PASMORE & C° T. Fox & Co.
Sheffield
1784

FREETH H. Freeth
Birmingham
1816

 Frogatt, Coldwell &
Lean
Sheffield
1797

Michael Hunter & Son
Talbot Works, Sheffield

Arthur E. Furniss
Sheffield
1859 ...

A.E. FURNISS
SHEFFIELD

John Batt & Co.
London

 John Grinsell & Henry Bourne *Birmingham* 1864–1871

 J. Green *Sheffield*

 G. & J. Bushell *Birmingham* 1899 ...

 Gilbert & Spurrier Ltd *Birmingham*

 Gilbert & Spurrier Ltd *Birmingham* 1886 ...

 R. Gainsford *Sheffield* 1808

 Alfred Field & Co. *Birmingham &* *Sheffield*

   George Bishop & Sons *Sheffield* 1890 c. ...

 George Bowen & Son Birmingham 1877–1890

George Bishop & Sons
Sheffield
1894–1940

Gotscher & Co.
Birmingham

Gotscher & Co.
Birmingham

G. Deakin & Co.
Sheffield

G.E. Hawkins
Birmingham
1887 ...

George Hawksley &
Co.
Sheffield

G. Harrison
Birmingham
1823

G. Harrison
Sheffield
1823

George Hawksley & Co.
Sheffield
1864 ...

George Hawksley & Co.
Sheffield

G. Lee & Co.
Sheffield
1888–1967

George Richmond
Collis & Co.
Birmingham
1848–1868

George Richmond
Collis & Co.
Birmingham
1869 c.–1893

George Shadford Lee
Sheffield
1879–1900 c.

George Goodfellow &
Sons
London
1882 ...

G. Teasdell
London

George Travis & Co.
Sheffield
1863 ...

G. Unite
Birmingham

G

George Ward
Sheffield

George Wish
Sheffield
1879 ...

R. Gainsford
Sheffield
1808 (OSP)

W. Garnett
Sheffield
1803 (OSP)

John Blyde
*Clintock Works,
Sheffield*

G. Gibbs
Birmingham
1808 (CP)

William Gibson & Co.
Ltd.
Belfast
1896 ...

GIBSON&Co L?
BELFAST

J. Gilbert
Birmingham
1812 (CP)

J. Gilbert
Birmingham
1812 (CP)

 J. Gilbert
Birmingham
1812 (CP)

 John Gangee
*The Glaciarium,
Middlesex*

 Edwin Lander & Co.
Birmingham

 N.C. Reading & Co.
Birmingham

 Edwin Fear
Bristol

 Goldsmiths' Alliance
Ltd
London

 The Goldsmiths &
Silversmiths Co. Ltd
London
1898 ...

 Goodman, Gainsforth
& Fairbairn
Sheffield
1800 (OSP)

 E. Goodwin
Sheffield
1795 (OSP)

Spurrier & Co.
London

J.G. Graves
Sheffield
1900–1914

J. G. GRAVES

E P N S   S

Benjamin Grayson & Son
Sheffield
1871 ...

**B.GRAYSON&SON
SHEFFIELD**

R. & J. Walsham
Birmingham

**THE
GREAT EASTERN**

J. Green
Birmingham
1807

J. Green & Co.
Birmingham
1799

W. Green & Co.
Sheffield
1784

Barker Brothers
Birmingham

CRIEL NICKEL SILVER

Griffiths & Browett
Birmingham
1862

Doughty, Alexander & Co.
Liverpool

J. & J. Drysdale & Co.
London

I. Guide & Co.
Sheffield
1895 c. ...

D. & G. Holy
Sheffield
1821

Harold & Ashwin
Birmingham
1868 ...

Hukin & Fenton
Birmingham

Jonathan Wilson Hukin
& John Thomas Heath
Birmingham
1875 ...

Joseph Hirons &
Henry Hodson Plante
Birmingham
1860–1863

W. Hutton
Sheffield
1839

William Hutton & Sons
Sheffield & London

William Hutton & Sons
Sheffield & London

William Hutton & Sons
Sheffield & London

Archer & Company
Sheffield

 Archer, Machin &
Marsh
Sheffield

 Henry Atkin
Sheffield
1823

 Atkin Brothers
Sheffield
1868 ...

 Atkin Brothers
Sheffield
1853 ...

 Henry Bourne
Birmingham
1896 ...

 Harrison Brothers &
Howson
Sheffield
1862–1909

 Harrison Brothers &
Howson
Sheffield
1862 c.–1896

 Harrison Brothers &
Howson
Sheffield
1897 ...

55

Haseler Brothers
Birmingham
1884–1887

Hammond, Creake & Co.
Sheffield
1886–1935

HC&C₀S
5856

Hawksworth, Eyre &
Co.
Sheffield
1850 c.–1873

Hawksworth, Eyre &
Co.
Sheffield
1853–1867

Hawksworth, Eyre &
Co. Ltd.
Sheffield
1874 ...

Hawksworth, Eyre &
Co.
Sheffield
1892–1894

Hawksworth
Sheffield
1894–1911

Harrison Fisher
Sheffield
1898 ...

H. Freeth
Birmingham
1816

H. Fisher & Co.
Sheffield
1900–1920

H.G. Long & Co.
Sheffield
1890 c. ...

Harrison Brothers &
Howson
Sheffield

Harrison Brothers &
Howson
Sheffield

Henry Hall
Birmingham
1829

Walker
Sheffield
1868–1916

Henry Hobson & Sons
Sheffield & London
1889 c. ...

Henry Hodson Plante
& Co.
Birmingham
1882–1896

James Howarth & Sons
Sheffield

Henry Millington Harwood
& Henry Holdson Plante
Birmingham
1887–1892

Hardman, Powell & Co.
Birmingham
1883 …

Boardman
Sheffield
1861–1927

Harwood, Plante &
Harrison
Birmingham
1883–1886

Joseph Hirons, Henry
Hodson Plante & Co.
Birmingham
1863–1882

Henry Rogers, Sons &
Co.
Sheffield
1897 …

H. Schurhoff & Co.
Birmingham

Tudor & Leader
Sheffield
1760 (OSP)

Tudor & Leader
Sheffield
1760 (OSP)

	Horace Woodward & Co. *Birmingham* 1876–1893
	Henry Wilkinson & Co. Ltd *Sheffield* 1872–1892
	Henry Wilkinson & Co. *Sheffield* 1862 c.–1872
	Henry Wilkinson & Co. *Sheffield* 1843–1871
	Henry Wilkinson & Co. Ltd *Sheffield* 1872–1894
	Henry Wilkinson & Co. Ltd *Sheffield* 1872–1894
	Horace Woodward & Co. Ltd *Sheffield* 1894 …
	W. Hall *Birmingham* 1820
	George Walker & Henry Hall *Sheffield* 1891 c. …

W. Hall
Birmingham
1820
(CP)

Joseph Hancock
Sheffield
1755
(OSP)

**IOSᴴ HANCOCK
SHEFFIELD.**

M. Hanson
Sheffield
1810
(OSP)

G.W. Harris & Co.
Sheffield
1845–1863

**G.W. HARRIS & Cᴼ
SHEFFIELD**

J. Harrison
Sheffield
1809
(OSP)

Harrison
Sheffield
1843–1865

HARRISON
NORFOLK WORKS
SHEFFIELD
2746

Harrison & Howson
Sheffield
1862–1909

James Dixon & Sons,
Harrods
Sheffield & London
1890 c. ...

Henry Millington
Harwood & Son
Birmingham
1892–1894

	Aaron Hatfield *Sheffield* 1808 c. (OSP)
	Aaron Hatfield *Sheffield* 1810 c. (OSP)
G & J W HAWKSLEY	George Hawksley & Co. *Sheffield* 1852 c.–1879 c.
SOLE PROPRIETORS **PERFECTION** SOLE PROPRIETORS	Hayman & Company *Birmingham*
	Joseph Haywood & Co. *Sheffield* 1890 c. ...
	Henry Brooks & Co. *London*
HERALD **TRUMPETER**	C.A.E. Speyer & Co. *London*
HESSIN.	Andrew Charles *Birmingham*
	S. Hibbert & Son *Sheffield* 1900–1909

William Marples &
Sons
Sheffield

Higginson Robinson
Liverpool

D. Hill & Co.
Birmingham
1806   (CP)

J. Hinks
Birmingham
1812   (CP)

J. Hipkiss
Birmingham
1808   (CP)

J. Hobday
Birmingham
1829   (CP)

Henry Holdsworth &
Sons
Sheffield
1864–1900

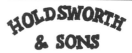

H. Holland & Co.
Sheffield
1784   (OSP)

D. & G. Holly
Sheffield
1821   (OSP)

	Dan Holly, Parker & Co. *Sheffield* 1804
	Dan Holly, Wilkinson & Co. *Sheffield* 1784
	H.H. Vivian & Co. Ltd. *Birmingham*
	J. Horton *Birmingham* 1809
	D. Horton *Birmingham* 1808
	S. & T. Howard *London* 1809
HOWARD SHEFFIELD	Francis Howard *Sheffield* 1890 c. ...
HUNTER SHEFFIELD	Michael Hunter & Sons *Sheffield* 1884–1887
	W. Hutton *Birmingham* 1807

W. Hutton
Birmingham
1837   (CP)

W. Hutton
Birmingham
1831   (CP)

I. & I. Waterhouse
Sheffield
1833

 John Bell
Sheffield

 Creswick & Co.
Sheffield
1858–1863

   John Gilbert
Birmingham
1876 ...

 Joseph Hancock
Sheffield
1755

 J. Harrison & Co.
Sheffield
1866–1891

 G. Lees
Birmingham
1811

 J. Knowles & Son
Sheffield

 John Littlewood
Sheffield
1772

Mappin & Co.
Royal Cutlery Works,
Sheffield

John Oxley
Sheffield

J.P. Cutts
Sheffield

J. Rowbotham & Co.
Sheffield
1768   (OSP)

Israel Sigmund
Greenberg & Co.
Birmingham
1895 ...

John Winter & Co.
Sheffield
1765   (OSP)

Frederick Whitehouse
Lion Works,
Birmingham

Imperial
F.W.

Frederick Whitehouse
Lion Works,
Birmingham

Imperial Silver
F.W.

N.C. Reading & Co.
Birmingham

Daniel & Arter
*Globe Nevada Silver
Works, Birmingham*

Perry & Company Ltd
Birmingham

Walter J. Ramsbottom
Vine Works, Sheffield

 IXION

G.E. Walton & Co. Ltd
Birmingham

James & Charles
Tidmarsh
London
1886 c.–1899

J. & J. Bell
Sheffield

John Biggin
Sheffield

Biggin, John
Sheffield

J. Bradbury
Sheffield
1889–1892

John Bodman
Carrington
London
1880 ...

J.B. Chatterley & Sons
Ltd.
Birmingham
1896 ...

Thomas Bradbury &
Sons
Sheffield
1863–1867

Jonas & George Bowen
Birmingham
1859–1877

Jonathan Bell & Son
Sheffield
1897 c. ...

Jonas Bowen & Sons
Birmingham
1877 ...

Thomas Bradbury &
Sons
Sheffield

James Chesterman &
Co. maker of
measuring tapes
Sheffield 1862 ...

J. Collyer & Co. Ltd
Birmingham
1900 ...

John Clarke & Sons
Sheffield
1895 ...

Creswick
Sheffield
1853–1855

Johnson, Durban &
Co. Ltd
Birmingham
1897 ...

James Deakin & Sons
Sheffield
1871–1890 c.

James Deakin & Sons *Sheffield* 1871–1898	
James Deakin & Sons *Sheffield* 1890 c. ...	
James Dixon & Sons *Sheffield* 1869 c.–1879 c.	
James Dixon & Sons *Sheffield* 1879 ...	
James Dixon & Sons *Sheffield*	
James Dixon & Sons *Sheffield* 1848 c.–1869 c.	
James Dixon & Sons *Sheffield* 1848–1878	1313
James Dixon & Sons *Sheffield* 1848–1878	190 W J
James Dixon & Sons *Sheffield* 1879–1935 c.	 2447 1/4

J.E. Bushell
Birmingham
1891 ...

 Joseph Elliot & Sons
Sheffield
1890 c. ...

 James Fenton
Birmingham

 James Fenton
Sheffield

 James Fenton
Sheffield
1868–1875

 James Fenton
Sheffield
1875–1883

 Joseph Gilbert
Sun Works,
Birmingham

 John Gough
Birmingham
1870–1885 c.

 John Gilbert & Sons
Birmingham &
London
1894 ...

John Grinsell & Sons
Birmingham
1892 …

John Harrison
Sheffield
1843–1866

John Hardman & Co.
Birmingham
1845–1875

John Hoyland & Co.
Sheffield
1764   (OSP)

J.H. Hunt
Birmingham
1887–1898

J. Hawksworth
Sheffield
1867–1911

J.H. Hunt & Co.
Birmingham
1898 …

T. & J. Creswick
Sheffield
1811   (OSP)

John Hoyland
Sheffield
1764   (OSP)

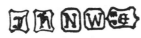

Harrison
Sheffield
1843–1865

Potter
Sheffield
1884–1890

J. Slate & Son
Sheffield

Hale Brothers
Sheffield

Hawksworth
Sheffield
1873–1892

Hawksworth
Sheffield
1873–1892

Mappin & Son
Sheffield

J. M. & Co.

John Morton & Co.
Sheffield & London

J. Needham
Sheffield

J. North
Sheffield

John Neal & Co.
London
1873–1880 c.

John Neal & Co.
London

J. Nodder
Sheffield
1890 c.–1904

John Nowill & Sons
Sheffield
1867–1889

James Pinder & Co.
Sheffield
1890 c. ...

James Pinder & Co.
Sheffield
1877–1894

J. Roberts
Sheffield

Joseph Rodgers & Sons
Sheffield

Joseph Rodgers & Sons
Sheffield

 John Round & Son Ltd
*Tudor & Arundel
Works, Sheffield*

 Joseph Rodgers & Sons
Sheffield
1822 (OSP)

 Joseph Rodgers & Sons
Sheffield
1822

  Joseph Rodgers & Sons
Sheffield
1858–1871

 Joseph Rodgers & Sons
Sheffield
1871 …

    John Round & Sons
Ltd
Sheffield
1863–1897

   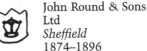 John Round & Sons
Ltd
Sheffield
1874–1896

 John Round & Sons
Ltd
Sheffield
1880 c.–1896

John Round & Sons
Ltd
Sheffield
1897 ...

John Round & Sons
Ltd
Sheffield
1872–1957

John Round & Sons
Ltd
*Tudor & Arundel
Works, Sheffield*

Josephus Smith
Sheffield

J. Smallwood
Sheffield
1823

J. Dixon
Sheffield
1848–1878

Jacob & Samuel
Roberts
Sheffield
1765

John Sherwood & Sons
Birmingham
1858–1896

John Sherwood & Sons
Birmingham
1897 ...

J. Thompson
Sheffield

 J. Thompson
Sheffield

 J. Turton & Co.
Sheffield
1898–1909

 J. Turton & Co.
Sheffield
1910–1923

 James Tidmarsh
London

 J. Townroe
Sheffield
1887–1916

 J. Turton & Co.
Sheffield
1898–1923

 Towndrow Brothers
Sheffield

 W. F. Wostenholme
Sheffield

Joseph Wilmore
Birmingham
1807

James Walter Tiptaft
Birmingham
1886 ...

J. Y. Cowlishaw
Sheffield

John Yates & Sons
Birmingham

J Y & S

John Yates & Sons
Birmingham
1879 ...

John Yates & Sons
Birmingham

John Yates & Sons
Birmingham

Daniel & Arter
*Globe Nevada Silver
Works, Birmingham*

James Jay
London
1867–1897

JAY
366 ESSEX ROAD
LONDON

C. JOHNSON & CO. SHEFFIELD	Cristopher Johnson & Co. *Sheffield* 1896 ...
	J. Johnson *Sheffield* 1812
	Jones *Birmingham* 1824
	T. Jordan *Sheffield*

Alfred F. Kleinwort &
Percy W. Peerless
London
1895–1896

Alfred F. Kleinwort &
Percy W. Peerless
London
1897 ...

Levetus Brothers
Birmingham

Kendal & Dent
London
1883 ...

Levetus Brothers
Birmingham

S. Kirkby
Sheffield
1812

Kirby, Beard & Co. Ltd
Birmingham &
Redditch
1897 ...

Lingard & Baker
Birmingham
1871 ...

Lee & Middleton
Sheffield

George Shadford Lee &
Henry Wigfull
Sheffield
1871–1898

George Shadford Lee &
Henry Wigfull Ltd
Sheffield
1899 ...

George Shadford Lee &
Henry Wigfull
Sheffield
1879–1898

Levesley Brothers
*Central Works,
Sheffield*

Levesley Brothers
*Central Works,
Sheffield*

Lockwood Brothers Ltd
Sheffield

Levesley
Sheffield
1875 c.–1935

Levesley
Sheffield
1875 c.–1935

J. Law & Son
Sheffield
1807   (OSP)

John Law
Sheffield
1810 c.   (OSP)

R. Law
Sheffield
1807   (OSP)

Thomas Law
Sheffield
1758   (OSP)

Thomas Law
Sheffield
1758   (OSP)

Thomas Law
Sheffield
1758   (OSP)

Daniel & Arter
*Globe Nevada Silver
Works, Birmingham*

A. C. Lea
Sheffield
1808   (OSP)

 Lee, White & Co.
Sheffield
1886–1887

 George Lees
Birmingham
1811 c.

LEES! George Lees
Birmingham
1811

LEVIATHAN. John James & Sons
*Victoria Works,
Redditch*

LIFE Francis John Townsend
Sheffield

 John Lilly
Birmingham
1815

 Joseph Lilly
Birmingham
1816

LINDER FEARNLEY
SHEFFIELD
Linder Fearnley
Sheffield
1851–1852

**ALFRED LINDLEY
SHEFFIELD**
Alfred Lindley
Sheffield
1883–1896

M. Linwood & Sons
Birmingham
1808   (CP)

J. Linwood
SBirmingham
  (CP)
1807

J. Linwood
Birmingham
1807   (CP)

W. Linwood
Birmingham
1807   (CP)

Michael Hunter & Son
Talbot Works, Sheffield

Lockwood Brothers Ltd.
Sheffield
1898 c. ...

J. Love & Co. and
Love, Silverside, Darby
& Co.
Sheffield 1785 c.   (OSP)

Love, Silverside, Darby
& Co.
Sheffield
1785 c.   (OSP)

 Joseph Mappin &
Brothers
Sheffield

 Mackay & Chisholm
Edinburgh

  Joshua Maxfield &
Sons
Sheffield
1894 ...

 Mappin & Webb
Sheffield & London
1897 c. ...

 Mappin Brothers
*Queens Works,
Sheffield & London*

 Mappin Brothers
*Queens Works,
Sheffield & London*

 M. Beal
Sheffield

 McLean Brothers &
Rigg Ltd
London

 William Mammat,
George Albert Buxton
& Co.
Sheffield 1865–1867

85

Richard Morton
Sheffield
1765

Richard Morton
Sheffield
1765

M. de J. Levy & Sons
London

Richard Martin
Sheffield
1854–1897

Richard Martin,
Ebenezer Hall & Co.
Sheffield
1854 ...

Richard Martin,
Ebenezer Hall & Co.
Sheffield
1860 c.–1896

Richard Martin
Sheffield
1880–1934

Richard Martin,
Ebenezer Hall & Co.
Sheffield
1895 c. ...

James McEwan & Co.
Ltd
London

Mappin, Webb & Co.
Sheffield

Mappin, Webb & Co.
Sheffield
1861–1890

Willis
Sheffield
1872–1885

**HERBERT MACLAURIN
SHEFFIELD**

Herbert Maclaurin
Sheffield
1894 …

F. Madin & Co.
Sheffield
1788

Fisher
Sheffield
1900–1925

Mappin Brothers
Sheffield
1848–1863

MAPPIN BROS

Mappin Brothers
*Queens Works,
Sheffield & London*

Mappin Brothers
Sheffield
1865–1905

Mappin Brothers *Sheffield* 1850	
Mappin Brothers Sheffield 1863–1894 c.	**MAPPIN·BROTHERS** **222.REGENT STREET** **AND** **LONDON-BRIDGE**
John Newton Mappin & George Webb *Sheffield & London* 1866–1871	**MAPPIN&WEBB** **77&78OXFORD ST** **71&72CORNHILL** **LONDON**
John Newton Mappin & George Webb *Sheffield & London* 1871–1880 c.	**MAPPIN&WEBB** **76,77&78OXFORD ST** **&MANSIONHOUSE** **BUILDINGS.CITY** **LONDON**
Mappin & Webb *Sheffield* 1887 …	MAPPIN & WEBB'S **PRINCE'S PLATE,** R⁹ 71552
Mappin & Webb *Sheffield & London* 1887 c. …	**MAPPIN&WEBB** **PRINCES'PLATE**
Mappin & Webb Ltd. *Sheffield & London* 1899 c. …	**MAPPIN&WEBB'S** **PRINCES PLATE** **LONDON & SHEFFIELD**
Mappin & Webb *Sheffield* 20th Century	MAPPIN & WEBB London & Sheffield MAPPIN PLATE ⬚ W 20252 ⅙ PINT
W. Markland *Sheffield* 1818	**W·MARKLAND**

 Bramwell, Brownhill & Co.
Sheffield

 MATTHIAS SPENCER & SONS Spencer, Matthias & Sons
Sheffield

 S. Maw, Son & Thompson
London

 Samuel Hancock & Sons
Mazeppa Works, Sheffield

 H. Meredith
Sheffield
1807

 John Baker & Company
Wheeldon Works, Sheffield

 MEXICAN SILVER James Tidmarsh
London

 George Bishop & Sons
Sheffield
1890 c. ...

 **MIXITINE** Swann & Adams
Canada Works, Birmingham

J. Moore
Sheffield
1784   (OSP)

J. Moore
Sheffield
1784   (OSP)

F. Moore
Sheffield
1820   (OSP)

Lockwood Brothers Ltd
Sheffield

S. Mordan & Co.
London

R. Morton & Co.
Sheffield
1785   (OSP)

H.D. Muir & Co.
London

John Neal & Co.
London

 Platnauer Brothers
Bristol

 Nathaniel Smith
Sheffield
1756

N.W. Norton & White
Birmingham
1883–1899

   Needham, Veall &
Tyzack
Sheffield
1890 c. ...

 W.S. Savage & Co.
Sheffield

NEAL'S PYRO SILVER John Neal & Co.
London

 C. Needham
Sheffield
1821

 William Milner &
Sons
Leek

Henry Wilkinson &
Co. Ltd
Sheffield

Daniel & Arter
*Globe Nevada Silver
Works, Birmingham*

F.R. Martino
Birmingham

W. Newbould & Son
Sheffield
1804 (OSP)

John McLeownan
McMurtrie
Glasgow

J. Nicholds
Sheffield
1808 (OSP)

Matthias Spencer &
Sons
Sheffield
1880 c. ...

John Nodder & Sons
Sheffield
1863 ...

John Nodder & Sons
Sheffield
1863–1904

	Osborn & Elliot *Sheffield*
	T. Oldham *Sheffield* 1860
	Slack & Grinold *Bath Works, Sheffield*
	H. Schurhoff & Co. *Birmingham*
T. OTLEY **SHEFFIELD**	Thomas Otley & Co. *Sheffield* 1846 c.–1860
THOMAS OTLEY **SHEFFIELD**	Thomas Otley & Co. *Sheffield* 1861–1875
THOMAS OTLEY **& SONS** **SHEFFIELD**	Thomas Otley & Sons *Sheffield* 1876–1888

Pembrook & Dingley
Birmingham
1883–1886

Pembrook & Dingley
Birmingham
1887–1898

Parkin & Marshall
Telegraph Works,
Sheffield

Philip Ashberry &
Sons
Sheffield
1856–1890 c.

Philip Ashberry &
Sons
Sheffield
1861–1890

Philip Ashberry &
Sons
Sheffield
1880 c. ...

Philip Ashberry &
Sons
Sheffield
1867–1935

Philip Ashberry &
Sons
Sheffield
1880–1935

Philip Ashberry &
Sons
Sheffield

Payton & Co.
Birmingham

Padley, Parkin & Co.
Sheffield

Padley, Parkin &
Staniforth
Sheffield
1855 c.–1880 c.

J. Prime
Birmingham
1839

Padley, Staniforth &
Co.
Sheffield

The Potosi Silver Co.
Birmingham
1878 …

Pryor, Tzack & Co.
Sheffield

Walker & Hall
Sheffield

**RICHARD PARKIN
& SON
SHEFFIELD**

Richard Parkin & Son
Sheffield
1853–1872

Thomas Parkin
Sheffield
1839–1871

J. Parsons & Co.
Sheffield
1784 (OSP)

L. & C. Glauert
Sheffield

Pinder Brothers
Sheffield
1923–present

Peake
Sheffield
1807 (OSP)

A. & F. Pears
London & Middlesex

R. Pearson
Sheffield
1811 (OSP)

Pemberton & Mitchell
Sheffield
1817 (OSP)

Hawksworth, Eyre &
Co.
Sheffield

Hands & Sons
Birmingham

 Jackson Petfield
Sheffield
1876

 C. Jones
Liverpool

  Samuel Pimley
Birmingham
1810 c.

 Piston Freezing
Machine & Ice Co.
Middlesex

 John Derby & Sons
Sheffield

 The Potosi Silver Co.
Birmingham

 The Potosi Silver Co.
Birmingham

 Potter
Sheffield
20th Century

John Henry Potter *Sheffield* 1884 ...		
J. Prime *Birmingham* 1839 (CP)		
J. Prime *Birmingham* 1839 (CP)		
J. Prime *Birmingham* 1839 (CP)		
Thomas Prime & Son *Birmingham* 1844 c.–1894		
Thomas Prime & Son *Birmingham*		
John Neal & Co. *London*	**PYRO GOLD**	

 Samuel Roberts & Charles Belk
Sheffield
1863 ...

 Roberts & Briggs
Sheffield

 Rose & Brough
Birmingham
1894 ...

   Roberts
Sheffield
1864–1867

 Roberts
Sheffield
1864–1867

 Roberts
Sheffield
1892–1920 c.

 Roberts & Briggs
Sheffield
1860

 Roberts
Sheffield
1916–1919

 Roberts
Sheffield
1920–1923

Roberts & Hall
Sheffield

Roberts & Slater
Sheffield

Samuel Roberts &
Joseph Slater
Sheffield
1845–1858

Roberts Smith & Co.
Sheffield
1828

Rhodes Brothers
Sheffield

William Hutton &
Sons
Sheffield & London

A. Hodd & Sons
Middlesex

Richard Hodd & Son
London
1872–1896

Martin, Hall & Co.
*Shrewsbury Works,
Sheffield*

R.M. Johnson & Co.
Sheffield
1890 c. ...

 R.M. Johnson & Co.
*Shoreham Plate Works,
Sheffield*

    Robert Pringle & Co.
London
1882 ...

 Richard Richardson
Sheffield
1873–1900 c.

 Richard Richardson
Sheffield
1895 ...

 Richard Richardson
Sheffield
1873–1924

  Rylands
Sheffield
1876–1910 c.

     Ridge, Woodcock & Hardy
Sheffield
18765–1880

 W.R. Humphreys & Co.
Sheffield

Willaim Daffern
Birmingham

Openshaw & Co.
Birmingham &
London

John Ridal
Paxton Works, Sheffield

RAINBOW

Frederick Barnes & Co.
London, Birmingham
& Sheffield

John Sherwood & Sons
Birmingham

Bramwell, Brownhill &
Co.
Sheffield
1891 ...

Frederick Derry
Birmingham
1867–1891

Theophilus Richards
& Co.
Birmingham

 THEOPHILUS RICHARDS & Co

Richard Richardson
Sheffield
1873–1900 c.

**R. RICHARDSON
CORNWALL WORKS
SHEFFIELD**

Joseph Ridge & Co.
Sheffield
1880–1884

Roberts Cadman & Co.
Sheffield
1785

J. S. Roberts
Sheffield
1786   (OSP)

Joseph Rodgers & Sons
Sheffield
1822   (OSP)

RODGERS

Joseph Rodgers & Sons
Sheffield

RODGERS
CUTLERS
TO HER
MAJESTY

ORIGINAL & GENUINE PLATE

Joseph Rodgers & Sons
Sheffield

Joseph Rodgers & Sons
Sheffield

JOSEPH RODGERS & SONS

Joseph Rodgers & Sons
Sheffield

V ♛ R
JOSEPH RODGERS &SONS
CUTLERS TO HER MAJESTY.
✳ ✠

Joseph Rodgers & Sons
Sheffield

Joseph Rodgers & Sons
Sheffield
1860–1970

Joseph Rodgers & Sons
Sheffield

RODGERSINE

Joseph Rogers & Sons
Birmingham   (CP)
1819

ROGERS

Henry Rogers, Sons & Co.
Sheffield
1897 ...

HENRY ROGERS, SONS & C$\underline{o}$
CUTLERS SHEFFIELD

Rosing Brothers & Co.
London

Frederick Derry
Birmingham

"ROYAL STANDARD"

Frederick Derry
Birmingham

"ROYAL STANDARD"
VICTORIA
SILVER

W. Ryland & Son
Sheffield   (OSP)
1807

RYLAND

John Nodder & Sons
Sheffield
1894 c. ...

 Sansom & Creswick
Sheffield

   Sansom & Creswick
Sheffield

 Arthur Elwell Spurrier
& Co.
London
1886 ...

 James Shaw & Fisher
Sheffield
1872–1894

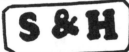 Slater, Son & Horton
Sheffield

 Stacey, Henry &
Horton
Sheffield

 Slack Brothers
Leicester Works,
Sheffield

    S. Bright & Co.
Sheffield

Sturges, Bladdon &
Middleton
Birmingham
1884 ...

S. Colmore
Sheffield
1790

Samuel Evans & Sons
Birmingham
1875 ...

Fenton
Sheffield
1888–1891

S.F. Evans & Co.
Birmingham
1894 ...

Fenton
Sheffield
1891–1896

S. & T. Howard
Sheffield
1809

Sheffield Plate Co.
Sheffield
1884

Roberts
Sheffield
1867–1879

 Fenton Mathews & Co.
Sheffield
1760 (OSP)

 Selig, Sonnenthal &
Co.
London

  Thomas Bradbury &
Sons
Sheffield
1858–1896

 W. & S. Ward
Manchester

 H. Samuel & Sons
Manchester

 Harriet Samuel
Sheffield
1880 c. ...

 T. Sansom & Sons
Sheffield
1821

SAVARS. Evans, Lescher &
Webb
London

SAVARS. Evans Sons & Co.
Liverpool

Adey Bellamy Savory
& Sons
London
1854–1866

Howell & James Ltd
London

The "Sceptre"

"Jubilee"

W. Scott
Birmingham
1807

James Shaw & Fisher
Sheffield
1833–1894

**SHAW & FISHER
SHEFFIELD**

James Shaw & Fisher
Sheffield
1872–1894

**SHAW&FISHER
43 SUFFOLK ROAD
SHEFFIELD**

Alfred R. Ecroyd
Sheffield
1884–1890

J. Shephard
Birmingham
1817

R. Binnall & Co.
Shrewsbury

Hawksworth, Eyre &
Co.
Sheffield

SIBERIAN SILVER Hawksworth, Eyre & Co.
Sheffield

 R. Silk
Birmingham
1809

 W. Silkirk
Birmingham
1807

 Potter
Sheffield
1884–1940

SILVENE Henry Fielding
Birmingham

 John Yates & Sons
Birmingham

 Maurice Baum
Sheffield

 Maurice Baum
Sheffield

 William Page & Co.
Birmingham

Arthur Heckford
Egerton
Birmingham

John Yates & Sons
Birmingham

John Yates & Sons
Birmingham

William Rae & Co.
Liverpool

John Ingram
Birmingham

W.R. Box & Co.
Dublin

Hutton
Sheffield
20th Century

T. Small
Birmingham
1812

I. Smith
Birmingham
1821

	W. Smith *Sheffield* 1812
	Smith & Co. *Sheffield* 1784
	Smith, Tate, Nicholson & Hoult *Sheffield* 1810
	J. Smith *Sheffield* 1836
	N. Smith & Co. *Sheffield* 1784
	J. Smith & Son *Sheffield* 1828
	Walker & Hall *Sheffield*
	Mason Brothers Ltd *London*
SOUTHERN & RICHARDSON SHEFFIELD	Southern & Richardson *Sheffield* 1887–1900 c.

111

Spencer, Matthias &
Sons
Sheffield

John Batt & Company
London

William Spurrier
Birmingham
1850 c.–1887

SPURRIER

Ebenezer Stacey &
Sons
Sheffield
1870 c.–1900 c.

**E. STACEY & SONS
SHEFFIELD**

Ebenezer Stacey
Sheffield
1843–1856

**E. STACEY
SUCCESSOR TO
I. VICKERS
BRITANNIA PLACE
SHEFFIELD**

Ebenezer Stacey & Son
Sheffield
1857–1900 c.

**STACEY
& SON
SUCCESSORS TO
JOHN VICKERS
BRITANNIA PLACE
SHEFFIELD**

George Wheeler
Birmingham

Frederick Derry
Birmingham

Frederick Derry
Birmingham

**"STANDARD"
VICTORIA
SILVER**

	Staniforth, Parkin & Co. *Sheffield* 1784
	William T. Staniforth *Ascend Works, Sheffield*
	Steam Electro-Plating & Gilding Co. *Southampton*
	Keep Brothers *Birmingham*
	B. Stot *Sheffield* 1811
SUNLIGHT	Lever Brothers *Port Sunlight*
	Muirhead, James & Co. *Glasgow*
	Sykes & Co. *Sheffield* 1784
SYLFERET.	Roberts & Belk *Furnival Works, Sheffield*

Thompson & Brown *Sheffield*	
T. Badger & Co. *Sheffield*	
Thomas Bradbury & Sons *Sheffield* 1867–1878	
Thomas Bradbury & Sons *Sheffield* 1858–1863	
Thomas Bradbury & Sons *Sheffield* 1892–1916	
Thomas Bradbury & Sons *Sheffield* 1853–1857	
T. Butts *Birmingham* 1807	
T.W. Eaton *Sheffield*	
T. Ellis *Plymouth*	

	T. Freeman *Sheffield*
	Thomas Goodfellow *London* 1873–1893
	Thomas Goodfellow *London* 1893 …
	Thomas Hardwood & Sons *Birmingham* 1864–1896
	Thomas Harwood *Birmingham* 1845–1864
	Creswick *Sheffield* 1852–1853
	Thomas Latham & Ernest Morton *Birmingham* 1866–1896
	Thomas Latham & Ernest Morton *Birmingham* 1897 …
	T. Land *Sheffield* 1901–1919

T. Marples
Sheffield

T.P. Lowe
Sheffield

Thomas Otley & Sons
Sheffield
1889 c.–1900

T. Royle
Sheffield

W.R. Nutt & Co.
Sheffield
1894 ...

Ridge, Woodcock &
Hardy
Sheffield

Thomas Turner
Sheffield

Thomas Turner & Co.
Suffolk Works,
Sheffield

Thomas Turner & Co.
Sheffield
1886 ...

 Thomas Turner & Co.
Sheffield
1865–1885 c.

 Thomas Thorold
Sturtevant
London
1871 ...

 Thomas Turner & Co.
Sheffield
1883–1940

 Tudor & Leader
Sheffield
1760

 Thomas Woolley
Birmingham
1887–1897

 Thomas Woolley
Birmingham
1898 ...

 Thomas Wilkinson &
Co.
Birmingham
1844 c.–1875 c.

 Thomas White & Co.
Birmingham
1893 ...

 Thomas Wilkinson &
Sons
Birmingham
1875 c. ...

Taunton & Johnnson
Birmingham
... 1885 c.

Needham, Veall &
Tyzack
*Eye Witness Works,
Sheffield*

Lloyd, Taylor & Co.
London

S. Thomas
Sheffield
1818

E. Thomason &
Dowler
Birmingham
1807

E. Thomason &
Dowler
Sheffield
1807

Tonks & Co.
Sheffield
1824

Samuel Tonks
Birmingham
1807

Albert Samuel Bradley
Sheffield

TOPAZ

	James Schoolbred & Co. *Middlesex*
	Aluminium Co. Ltd *London*
	Armstrong, Stevens & Son *Birmingham*
	Creswick *Sheffield* 1852–1890
	Daniel & Arter *Globe Nevada Silver Works, Birmingham*
	Gotscher & Company *Birmingham*
	William Mather *Manchester*
	Thomas Otley & Sons *Sheffield* 1889–1900 c.
	Planters' Stores & Agency Co. *London*

N.C. Reading & Co.
Birmingham

Roberts & Belk
Sheffield
1895–1920 c.

Van Wart, Son & Co.
Birmingham

Henry Barnascone &
Son
Sheffield
1884 ...

Levetus Brothers
Birmingham

Frederick Newton &
Co.
London

Thomas White
Birmingham

Mappin & Webb
Sheffield & London
1899 c. ...

Mappin
Sheffield
1873 ...

	Mappin *Sheffield* 1900 ...
	Newton, Francis & Sons *Portobello Works,* *Sheffield*
	Tudor, Leader & Nicholson *Sheffield* 1784
	S. Turley *Birmingham* 1816
	J. Turton *Birmingham* 1820
	J. Turton *Birmingham* 1820
	John Tyler *Sheffield* 1836–1869
	J. Tyndall *Birmingham* 1813

William Whiteley
Middlesex

UNIVERSAL PROVIDER.

Vale Brothers &
Sermon
Birmingham
1884 ...

 Van Wart, Son & Co.
Birmingham

VALARIUM John Round & Son
Ltd.
Tudor & Arundel
KENDULAM *Works, Sheffield*

 N.C. Reading & Co.
Birmingham

 Henry Rossell & Co.
Sheffield

 VENTURE Slater Brothers
Sheffield

 Phosphor Bronze Co.
Southwark, Surrey

George Waterhouse &
Co.
Sheffield

George Waterhouse &
Co.
Sheffield
1842

Wilson & Davis
London & Sheffield

Wilson & Davis
London & Sheffield

Watson
Sheffield
1897–1940

George Walker &
Henry Hall
Sheffield
1861 ...

George Walker &
Henry Hall
Sheffield
1862–1896

Walker
Sheffield
1861–1890

Walker
Sheffield
1852–1897

W. & M. Dodge
Manchester

George Waterhouse &
Co.
Sheffield

William Arthur Smith
Benson & Co.
London
1898 ...

W. Brearley
Sheffield

W. Briggs
Sheffield
1823

William Batt & Sons
Sheffield
1895 c. ...

W.C. Cox
Birmingham
1878 ...

William Clarke
London
1885–1888

W. & M. Dodge
Manchester

Perry & Company Ltd
Birmingham

W. E. W.

W.F. Casewell
Birmingham
1893 ...

W.F.C

W. F. Wostenholme
Sheffield

W.F.W

W.F. Wostenholme
Sheffield
1858–1870

W.F.W.

William Gallimore &
Co.
Sheffield

W.G

William Gallimore &
Co.
Sheffield
1864–1887

William Gough
Birmingham
1849–1870

William Hutton &
Sons
Sheffield & London

WH

William Henry Lyde
Birmingham
1881 ...

William Hutton &
Sons
Sheffield
1864–1886 c.

William Hutton &
Sons
Sheffield
1849

William Hutton &
Sons
Sheffield & London

William. Hutton
Sheffield
1849

William James Myatt
& Co.
Birmingham
1900 ...

Walker, Knowles & Co.
Sheffield

Lee, William & Sons
Sheffield

W. Morton
Sheffield

William Mammat &
Sons
Sheffield
1879–1895

William Marples &
Sons
Sheffield
1883 c.–1896

William Marples &
Sons
Sheffield
1897 ...

William Page & Co.
Birmingham
... 1896

Parkin & Marshall
Telegraph Works,
Sheffield

William Page & Co.
Birmingham

William Page & Co.
Birmingham
... 1896

William Page & Co.
Birmingham
1897 ...

Taylor & Company
Swansea

W.R. Humphreys &
Co.
Sheffield
1889 c. ...

	W.R. Nutt & Co. *Sheffield* 1894 ...
	William Sissons & George *Sheffield & London*
	William Spurrier & Co. *Birmingham* 1889 ...
	Sissons *Sheffield* 1858–1885
	Stratford, W & H *Sheffield*
	William Suckling & Sons *Birmingham* 1895 ...
	Shirtcliffe *Sheffield* 1921–1931
	Robert Pringle & Co. *Wilderness Works, Middlesex*
	W.W. Harrison & Co. *Montgomery Works, Sheffield*

W.W. Harrison & Co.
Montgomery Works,
Sheffield

W.W. Harrison & Co.
Montgomery Works,
Sheffield

William Wheatcroft
Harrison
Sheffield
1857–1896

White, Henderson &
Co.
Elcho Works, Sheffield

White & Johnstone
Sheffield

Walker & Hall
Sheffield
1878 c. ...

Walker & Hall
Sheffield
1893 c. ...

Walker & Hall
Sheffield
1891–1909

Walker & Hall
Sheffield
1910–1970

 J. Waterhouse & Co.
Sheffield
1807 ⓄⓈⓅ

 J. Waterhouse & Co.
Sheffield
1833 c. ⓄⓈⓅ

 Waterhouse, John,
Hatfield, Edward &
Co.
Sheffield 1836 c. ⓄⓈⓅ

 Watson, Fenton &
Bradbury
Sheffield
1795 ⓄⓈⓅ

 Watson, Pass & Co.
(Late J. Watson)
Sheffield
1811 ⓄⓈⓅ

WWATSON
MAKER
SHEFFIELD

W. Watson
Sheffield
1883 ⓄⓈⓅ

WATTS&HARTON
LONDON

Watts & Harton
London
1854 c. ...

WILLIAM WEBSTER
SYCAMORE WORKS

William Webster
Sheffield
1880 c. ...

 Bonser & Son
London

W

Francis Howard
Aberdeen Works,
Sheffield

John Blyde
Clintock Works,
Sheffield

W. Hipwood
Birmingham
1809

J. White & White &
Allgood
Birmingham
1811

Thomas White
Sheffield
1866–1892

William Whiteley
London
1885 c. ...

W. WHITELEY
WESTBOURNE GROVE
BAYSWATER

Wignall Heeley & Co.
Sheffield
1895 ...

WIGNALL HEELEY & CO.
SHEFFIELD

Henry Wilkinson &
Co.
Sheffield
1836 c.

Joseph Willmore
Birmingham
1807 c.

	Joseph Willmore *Sheffield* 1807
WITHIN THE REACH OF ALL.	Birts & Son *Woolwich*
	Needham, Veall & Tyzack *Sheffield* 1890 c. ...
	Needham, Veall & Tyzack *Eyewitness Works, Sheffield*
	W. Jervis *Sheffield* 1789
WOSTENHOLME & BIGGIN 117 MATILDA STREET SHEFFIELD	Wostenholme & Biggin *Sheffield* 1876–1879
	W. Woodward *Birmingham* 1814
	S. Worton *Birmingham* 1821
	J. Wright & G. Fairbairn *Sheffield* 1809

Ellis Newton
Birmingham

Parkin & Marshall
*Telegraph Works,
Sheffield*

John Copley & Sons
*Richmond Works,
Sheffield*

Henry Hobson & Sons
Sheffield & London
1889 c. ...

Y & S   John Yates & Sons
Birmingham

Y
V S   John Yates & Sons
Birmingham

YATES & SONS John Yates & Sons
Birmingham

YATES
VIRGINIAN SILVER   John Yates & Sons
Birmingham

YATES'S
VIRGINIAN   John Yates & Sons
Birmingham

   John Yates & Sons
Birmingham

J. YATES & SONS John Yates & Sons
Birmingham

 J **YATES** **&SONS**   John Yates & Sons
Birmingham

JOHN YATES & SONS John Yates & Sons
Birmingham

S. & C. Young & Co.
Sheffield
1813   (OSP)

Arrow

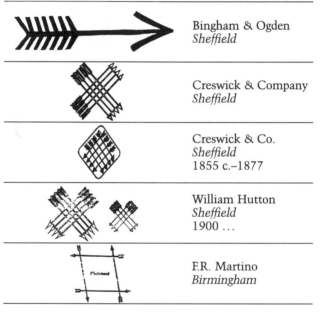

	Bingham & Ogden *Sheffield*
	Creswick & Company *Sheffield*
	Creswick & Co. *Sheffield* 1855 c.–1877
	William Hutton *Sheffield* 1900 …

F.R. Martino
Birmingham

Anchor

Wells, Gallimore &
Taylor
Birmingham

Bat

John Batt & Co.
London

Bell

Roberts, Smith & Co.
Sheffield
1828   (OSP)

William & George
Sissons
Sheffield
1858 …

Smith, Sissons & Co.
Sheffield
1848

Sissons
Sheffield
1858–1891

Belt

Charles Rowe
Courtney
Middlesex

Bird

	S. Brittain & Co. *St George's Works, Sheffield*
	Alfred Field & Co. *Birmingham & Sheffield*
	Alfred Field & Co. *Birmingham & Sheffield*
	Hukin & Heath *Birmingham*
	Ellis Newton *Birmingham*
	Jonathan Wilson Hukin & John Thomas Heath *Birmingham* 1889 c. ...
	The Potosi Silver Co. *Birmingham* 1878 ...
	Waterhouse Hatfield & Co. *Sheffield* 1886 (OSP)

Bird (cont.)

Thomas Wilkinson
Birmingham
1868 ...

Blacksmith

Charles Smith
Sheffield

Boar

J. & J. Beal
*Redhill Works,
Sheffield*

Boy

A. & F. Pears
London & Middlesex

Butterfly

John Morton & Co.
Sheffield & London

Centaur

Carl Maigatter
London

Compasses

William Jackson & Co.
*Sheaf Island Works,
Sheffield*

Cooper

Cooper Brothers &
Sons Ltd
Sheffield
1896 c. ...

Cross

Joseph Rodgers & Sons
Ltd.
Sheffield
1900 c. ...

Cupid

John Grinsell & Sons
Birmingham
1879 ...

John Grinsell & Sons
London

Deer

George Reid & Co.
London

Dragon

John Batt & Co.
London

Pictures

Dragon (cont.)

John Batt & Co.
London

Elephant

William Meyerstein &
Co.
London

Fan

Carl A. Von Der Mcden
London

Figure

John Batt & Co.
London

Henry Bourne
Birmingham
1877 ...

Figure (cont.)

John Dyson *Leeds*	
John S. Elmore & Co. *London*	
Speyer, Schwerdt & Co. *London*	

Fish

Not attributed 1760		

Flag

Philip Ashberry & Sons *Sheffield*	
Henry Rogers, Sons & Co. *Sheffield* ... 1896	

Fleur-de-Lys

	Atkin *Sheffield* 1890 ...
	William R. Deykin & Sons *Birmingham* 1892–1895
	William R. Deykin & Walter A. Harrison *Birmingham* 1895 ...
	Richard Hodd & William Linley *London* 1862–1872

Flower

	Maurice Baum *Sheffield* 1891 ...
	Rosing Brothers & Co. *London*
	Rosing Brothers & Co. *London*

Pictures

Globe

Daniel & Arter
Globe Nevada Silver
Works, Birmingham

Gong

James Deakin & Sons
Sheffield
1871–1900 c.

James Deakin & Sons
Sheffield
1890 c. …

Hand

Padley, Parkin & Co.
Sheffield
1849

Padley, Parkin & Co.
Sheffield
1849–1855 c.

Padley, Parkin &
Staniforth
Sheffield
1855 c.–1880 c.

Hand (cont.)

John Watson & Son
Sheffield
1830

Head

A. Hodd & Sons
Middlesex

Horn (Animal)

George Bowen & Sons
Birmingham
1890 c. ...

William Webster
Sheffield
1880 c. ...

Horn (Musical)

James Dixon & Sons
Sheffield
1879 ...

Pictures

Horn (Musical) (cont.)

James Dixon & Sons
Sheffield
1886 c. ...

James Dixon & Sons
Sheffield
1890 c. ...

Michael Hunter &
Sons
Sheffield
1884–1887

Horse

I. Guide & Co.
Sheffield
1895 c. ...

Hale Brothers
Sheffield
1885 c. ...

Hale Brothers
Sheffield

Moenich, Oscar & Co.
London

Pictures

Horse (cont.)

Henry Rogers & Sons
Co.
Sheffield &
Wolverhampton

Insect

Lewis Barnascone
Sheffield

Kangaroo

Robert Sorby & Sons
Sheffield
... 1898

Kettle

Joseph Haywood & Co.
Sheffield
1890 c. ...

Key

Atkin Brothers *Sheffield* 1895 c. ...	
Nowill, John & Sons *Sheffield*	
Henry Wilkinson & Co. *Sheffield* (OSP) 1836	
Henry Wilkinson & Co. *Sheffield* 1855 c.–1892	

Knight

S. Brittain & Co. *St George's Works,* *Sheffield*	
Henry Knight & Co. *London*	

Pictures

Lamp

Samuel Roberts &
Charles Belk
Sheffield
1863 ...

Lion

Charles Howard
Collins
Birmingham
1895 c. ...

Charles Howard
Collins
Birmingham

Koerber & Co.
London

Donald & Co.
Birmingham & Whitby

Oscar Moenich & Co.
London

Mermaid

Perry & Co. Ltd
Birmingham

Number

Robert Winter
Sheffield

Orb

Blagden, Hodgson
Sheffield
1821

Walker, Knowles & Co.
Sheffield
1840 (OSP)

Pipe

G. Wostenholm & Son
Ltd
*Washington Works,
Sheffield*

Plough

Samuel York & Co.
Wolverhampton

Scales

Meriden Britannia Co.
London

Sheep

Henry Brooks & Co.
London

Shield

Army & Navy Co-op
Society Ltd
Westminster

Philip Ashberry &
Sons
Sheffield
1880 ...

Shield (cont.)

R. Sutcliffe & Co.
Sheffield
1786

Thomas Hands
Birmingham
1899 ...

Signpost

William Suckling
Birmingham
1895 ...

Star

M. Boulton & Co.
Sheffield
1784

Frederick Whitehouse
Lion Works,
Birmingham

Pictures

Sun

	Arthur Egerton Heckford *Birmingham*
	Mappin Brothers *Sheffield* 1848–1863
	Mappin Brothers *Sheffield* 1863 …
	Mappin Brothers *Queens Works, Sheffield & London*

Sword

	Garfitt, Thomas & Son *Cross Scythes Works, Sheffield*
	Long, Hawksley & Co. *Hallamshire Works, Sheffield*
	H.G. Long & Co. *Sheffield* 1880 c. …

Sword (cont.)

Robert Pringle & Co.
London
1882 …

Target

Francis Howard
Sheffield
1890 …

Tree

Patrick O'Connor
Lancashire

Trident

Joseph Ridge & Co.
Sheffield
1880–1884

Joseph Ridge; John
Round & Sons Ltd
Sheffield
1886 …

Violin

George Ibberson
Sheffield

Wheatsheaf

Co-op Wholesale
Society Ltd
Manchester

Wheelbarrow

Henry Bolsover
*Portland Works,
Sheffield*

Others

Allen & Martin
Birmingham

Jonathan Bell
Sheffield

Others (cont.)

Charlton Brothers
Birmingham

John Goode & Sons
Birmingham

Gotscher & Co.
Birmingham

J.V. Hope &
G.F.W. Hope
*Atlantic Works,
Wednesbury & London*

Levy Brothers
London

J.S. Manton & Co.
Birmingham

Merzbach, Lang &
Fellheimer
London

John Nodder & Son
Sheffield

Others (cont.)

H. Schurhoff & Co.
Birmingham

Stacey Brothers
Sheffield

Taylor Brothers
*Adelaide Works,
Sheffield*

Walter Thornhill
Middlesex

Vernon's Patent China
& Glass Co. Ltd
London

James Vernon &
Brother
Wigtown

White & Ridsdale
London

John Wilson
Sheffield

Others (cont.)

Not attributed
Sheffield
1760